SUPERSTARS OF BASEBALL
JOSÉ REYES
THE RISE TO THE TOP!

He's a baseball superstar!

2012

Paid $105 million to play for the Miami Marlins for six years.

2011

Steals more bases and hits more triples than any other player in the National League.

2006

Plays in the Majors for the first time.

2003

Starts to play in the minors.

2000

Signs a contract with the New York Mets.

1999

Born in Villa González in the Dominican Republic.

1983

Mason Crest
370 Reed Road
Broomall, Pennsylvania 19008
www.masoncrest.com

Printed and bound in the United States of America.

First printing
9 8 7 6 5 4 3 2 1

Library of Congress Cataloging-in-Publication Data

Rodriguez Gonzalez, Tania.
 José Reyes / by Tania Rodriguez.
    p. cm.
 Includes index.
 ISBN 978-1-4222-2684-1 (hardcover) -- ISBN 978-1-4222-2670-4 (series) --
ISBN 978-1-4222-9173-3 (ebook)
 1. Reyes, José, 1983---Juvenile literature. 2. Baseball players--Dominican
Republic--Biography--Juvenile literature. I. Title.
  GV865.R4245R63 2013
 796.357092--dc23
 [B]
                                        2012020945

Produced by Harding House Publishing Services, Inc.
www.hardinghousepages.com

Picture Credits:
Daniel Padavona | Dreamstime.com: p. 4
Jerry Coli | Dreamstime.com: p. 27
Mangin, Brad: p. 2, 13, 16, 18, 19, 20, 24
MLB: p. 21, 28
NYSEG Stadium: p. 14
Paul Hakimata | Dreamstime.com: p. 12
Scott Anderson | Dreamstime.com: p. 22
slgckgc: p. 1

JOSÉ REYES

Chapter 1

BASEBALL, THE DOMINICAN REPUBLIC, AND JOSÉ REYES

Few baseball players have done the amazing things José Reyes has. In his *Major League Baseball (MLB)* career, Reyes seems to have done it all. He's played in the *World Series*. He's played in the *All-Star Game*. He's won awards and made millions of dollars. Reyes has broken records and set new ones. He's even been on the cover of a video game!

Superstars of Baseball: José Reyes

Palma Arriba, where José first started to play baseball.

Reyes worked hard to get where he is today. His journey to the Major Leagues began when he was very young. Growing up, Reyes dreamed of playing baseball for a living. Lots of little boys are like José Reyes used to be. All around the world, kids dream about playing baseball. They imagine themselves hitting a home run in a World Series game. For most kids, these are only dreams of course. But baseball has become a big part of life, in the United States, in Latin America, and in other places around the world. And it's not just little boys who get excited about baseball. Everyone loves baseball!

The Beginnings of Baseball

Where did baseball come from anyway? Actually, no one's really sure exactly how it was invented. But we do know that even though baseball as we know it today was first played in the United States, it really has roots in lots of different games played in Europe. In Russia, a game called *lapta* involved teams with pitchers and batters. In England, people played cricket and rounders, both games that have batters, pitchers, and two teams. Germans played town ball, which was even more similar to baseball, since players scored by running around a diamond.

Steroids

For many professional players, the pressure to perform well is intense. Athletes face stress from everyone around them to constantly improve their skill, strength, and speed in the game of baseball. Sometimes, an athlete turns to chemicals to reach a level of play that he wouldn't normally be able to achieve. This is never legal, and is almost always dangerous.

The most common performance enhancers are anabolic steroids. These chemicals are similar to testosterone, which is the male hormone naturally produced by the body to help stimulate muscle growth. That's why when a player takes anabolic steroids, he receives a boost to his speed and strength that is greater than what the body could normally do on its own. Major League Baseball, as well as almost every other organized sport, considers this cheating.

Steroids aren't good for you. They can raise your blood pressure. They can cause heart disease. Large doses of steroids can also lead to liver failure, and they sometimes cause problems similar to diabetes.

If an adolescent (typically someone under the age of about 17) takes anabolic steroids, the risks are often much worse. Steroids stop bones from growing, which results in stunted growth. In addition, the risks to the liver and heart are much greater, since a young person's liver and heart are not fully mature and are more easily damaged. Steroids can also cause emotional problems that usually start out with not being able to control anger.

Considering these health risks, as well as the fact that anabolic steroids are banned from organized sports, they should not be used, except by those who have a genuine medical condition that require their use.

Town ball and other games made their way to the United States during the 1700s and 1800s. By the early nineteenth century, people were playing a game that looked an awful lot like the baseball we play today.

The first recorded baseball team was formed in 1845. A man named Alexander Cartwright set up a team he called the New York Knickerbockers. Cartwright eventually wrote down some baseball rules. These rules are pretty familiar today: three strikes for each batter, three outs in an inning, umpires.

In 1869, the game turned *professional*. Before, people had come together to

Who Were the Alou Brothers?

FELIPE ALOU

In 1966, Felipe was named first baseman on the Sporting News All-Stars Team; he led the National League in total bases, hits, and at bats while also hitting 31 homers. Felipe was known for speaking up for Hispanics in the baseball world. Then, in 1979, Felipe became an Expos coach, and in 1992, he was named manager of the Expos. Two years later, in 1994, he was named Manager of the Year in the National League, and the next year he led the National League in the All-Stars game and took home the trophy.

MATTY ALOU

Felipe's brother Matty proved the baseball skill ran in the Alou family. Matty won the batting title in 1966 with .342; he posted a .338, .332, and .331 between 1967 and 1969. He even set a Major League record 698 official at-bats, and he retired with a .307 batting average.

JESÚS ALOU

Felipe and Matty's brother carried on the family baseball heritage. And on 10 September 1963, Jesús, Matty, and Felipe Alou all batted against the New York Mets in the same inning, the only time three Major League brothers have ever stepped up to the plate in the same inning! Between 1963 and 1979, Jesús had 82 pinch hits. His biggest day was on July 10, 1964, when he went six-for-six with five singles and a homer. In 1979, the Astros made Jesús a player-coach, and later he became a scout for the Montreal system in the Dominican Republic.

have fun and play a game. But as time went on, players got more serious. Some of them wanted to get paid. Slowly, each team started paying players.

Then leagues formed. Pretty soon, the two most important leagues were the National League and the American League, just like they are today.

In the 1920s, Babe Ruth became the best-known baseball star. He made the game even more popular. Fans went to games in cities across the United States. They could also listen to them on the radio. In 1947, Jackie Robinson became the first African American in the modern leagues.

Jesús, Matty, and Felipe Alou in 1963.

As the 1900s moved on, teams changed and were added. Rules changed. Games were aired on TV. Players got paid more and more, and some of them became superstars. Steroids became a problem, as some players illegally used them to get stronger and better. And baseball has traveled around the world!

All the Way to the Dominican Republic!

One place that baseball ended up is in the Dominican Republic. Most people think that Americans brought the game to Cuba first—and then Cubans brought it to the Dominican Republic when they fled their country during a war in the late 1800s.

Superstars of Baseball: José Reyes

The first Dominican teams popped up around 1895. The earliest teams included Los Tigres de Licey and Las Estrellas Orientales. Baseball's popularity grew and grew. The modern Dominican league started up in 1951.

Pretty soon, some Dominican players were catching the eye of Major League *scouts* from the United States. Players like Ozzie Virgil were *signed* to MLB teams. Players like the Alou brothers and Juan Marichal followed him.

Today, lots of people play baseball in the Dominican Republic. Kids grow up playing it on the local baseball field. People go to games to cheer for their favorite team. Many little boys dream of becoming professional baseball players themselves. They grow up surrounded by a rich baseball *culture.*

MLB teams and fans know that the Dominican Republic can produce great baseball stars. More baseball players come from the Dominican Republic than any other country in the world, besides the United States. In 2010, more than 10 percent of all the players in the MLB were Dominican. By 2011, a total of 420 players from the Dominican Republic had played in the Major Leagues.

One of those boys who dreamed of becoming a baseball star was José Reyes.

He drew on the strength of his country's baseball tradition to make it to the top. Now, he's living that dream. Today, Reyes is one of baseball's biggest stars. He's come a long way from the Dominican town where he was born!

José's Early Life

José Reyes was born on June 11, 1983 in Villa González in the Dominican Republic. José grew up in a small town outside Santiago called Palmar Arriba.

José's father's name was José Manuel. His mother's name was Rosa. José has a sister named Meosote, too.

José's family didn't have much money when he was growing up. They got by with the money they made from a little store right next to their house. The family didn't have a toilet in their house. They had to use an outhouse. When José started to play baseball, he didn't have a glove to play with. José learned to catch without a glove.

As a teenager, José became a better baseball player. He worked hard to learn what he could from other players. José played for a youth league team in Palmar Arriba.

In the summer of 1999, Reyes went to a New York Mets tryout camp in Santiago. There, scouts from the Mets saw how good Reyes was. Scouts Eddy

Toledo and Juan Mercado knew José could be a special player.

Eddy Toledo talked to the head of the Mets' international scouts. Toledo asked if he could sign the young José to a minor league contract. The team agreed, and Toledo talked to José and his family. The Mets offered José a contract to play in the *minor leagues*. José said yes. He gave half of the money he earned to his parents when he signed the *contract*. His family used the money to build a better house with indoor plumbing.

José had to work his way through the minor leagues before he could play in the Majors. But he was on his way to making his dream come true.

Chapter 2

STARTING IN BASEBALL

Most young players signed by the Mets go to the team's Dominican camp to train. When the team signed Reyes, they knew he could do even better. They knew he was good enough to go to the minors right away. They saw that he had a lot of potential.

To the Minors

In the 2000 season, Reyes played for the Kingsport Mets. Reyes was just 17 years old when he started playing for Kingsport. He played 49 games for the team in 2000. Reyes scored 22 runs and had 8 RBIs. Not bad for someone so young!

Reyes played shortstop in 40 games for Kingsport. His fielding percentage was .942. Reyes also helped make 20 double plays in 2000. He also played second and third base during the season.

He had shown the Mets that he could make it in the minors, so they kept him in. In 2001, the Mets moved Reyes to the Capital City Bombers. He played very well for the Bombers, doing even better than the year before. After the 2001 season, Reyes was named the New York Mets' minor league Player of the Year. People were starting to pay attention to him.

During the 2002 season, Reyes played for two teams. He started the season with the St. Lucie Mets. St. Lucie

José showed that he could play well early on.

plays in the Florida State League. After a few months, New York moved Reyes up to the Binghamton Mets. Binghamton is a Class AA team. Reyes played the rest of the season with the New York state team. He was already just one step away from the Majors.

Reyes played 65 games with Binghamton. His *batting average* was .287. He scored 46 runs and stole 27 bases. As shortstop, Reyes' fielding percentage was .940. He also won the New York Mets' minor league Player of the Year award again in 2002.

The Binghamton Mets' stadium in New York State, where Reyes played in 2002.

The Minor Leagues

Most baseball players don't go right from school to the Major Leagues. It's usually better when they can get some practice in the minor leagues first. The minor leagues operate in a bunch of countries, including Puerto Rico, the United States, Canada, Mexico, and the Dominican Republic.

Minor league teams form relationships with Major League teams. The Major Leagues look at the minor league players and decide who could play on their team. Sometimes the minor league teams are called "farm" teams. They "grow" players for the team they're connected to. Some of the relationships last a long time and some only last a couple years.

Playing in the Majors

Many people thought Reyes would start playing for the New York Mets at the beginning of 2003. He had won Player of the Year award twice, and was putting up some impressive numbers. The Mets signed Rey Sánchez to shortstop after the 2002 season, though. Reyes wouldn't move up at the start of the season after all.

In 2003, Reyes moved to a new minor league team. He started the season playing for the Norfolk Tides.

But then in June, Rey Sánchez was hurt. He couldn't play for the rest of the season. The Mets called Reyes and told him the news. They wanted him to replace Sánchez. He would be playing in the Majors! He'd be coming to New York to play for the Mets.

Reyes finished the 2003 season with his new team. He played his first Major League game one day before his 20th birthday.

In the 69 games he played with the Mets, Reyes scored 47 runs and had 32 RBIs. His batting average was .307. He also stole 13 bases. He helped make 42 double plays.

Reyes had made it to the Majors. He'd dreamed of playing baseball in the big leagues for years. Reyes had worked hard to make his way through the minor leagues. He'd played well each season and gotten better and better.

Finally, Reyes had his chance to play in the big leagues. And he was just 20 years old!

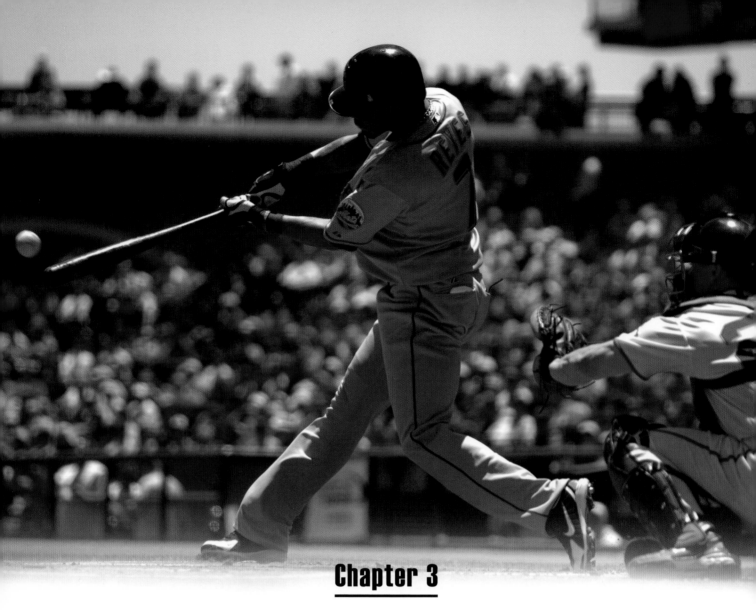

Chapter 3

PLAYING FOR
THE METS

Before the beginning of the 2004 season, the Mets signed another shortstop. Kazuo Matsui would only play shortstop. Reyes would have to change positions. The Mets moved Reyes to second base.

Reyes was hurt early on in the season. It was his first real injury in professional baseball. He couldn't play until late June. As a result, his batting average and fielding percentage dropped.

Near the end of the season, Reyes started playing shortstop again. Matsui moved to second base. Reyes' season hadn't been his best—but at least he was back to his favorite position.

In 2005, Reyes finally got his chance to play a full season with the Mets. And everyone agreed that it was a good one! It set him up for his next season.

A Big Year

Early in 2006, Reyes played for the Dominican Republic in the World Baseball Classic. He was known in multiple countries for being a talented player. In the first round, the Dominican Republic finished first. In the second round, the team finished first again. In the semi-finals, though, Cuba beat the Dominican Republic. Reyes scored one run and stole two bases.

In the 2006 MLB season, Reyes started strong. He won Player of the Week two weeks in a row in June. He was also chosen to be in the All-Star Game in 2006. Reyes was becoming more and more popular. Many fans in New York and around the world loved to watch Reyes play.

In August, the Mets signed Reyes to four more years. They didn't want to let him go. They thought he could help them get to the World Series. His contract would end after the 2010 season. They also had the option to extend his contract for another year.

During 2006, Reyes scored 122 runs and had 81 RBIs. He also hit 19 home runs. His batting average was .300. As shortstop, Reyes helped make 72 double plays. His fielding percentage was .971. At the end of the regular season, Reyes won his first Silver Slugger Award for his great playing.

Reyes helped the Mets achieve a lot during the 2006 season. His team finished first in the National League East. The Mets headed into the post-season. Reyes had never played in the post-season before, but now was his chance.

The Mets first played the Los Angeles Dodgers in the National League *Division* Series (NLDS). The Mets won and moved on to the National League Championship Series (NLCS). In the NLCS, the Mets played the St. Louis Cardinals. The series went on for seven games. In the end, the Mets lost to the Cardinals. Reyes' first post-season was over, but it had been exciting.

Reyes had had a huge year in 2006. No player in the National League stole

José Reyes as a shortstop.

more bases in 2006 than Reyes. No player in the NL hit more triples than Reyes. Reyes had only been in the Majors for two full seasons. But his numbers were some of the best in baseball! Everyone knew he was a player to watch closely.

Reyes broke his team's record for stolen bases.

Chapter 4

STAYING IN NEW YORK

T he fans knew that Reyes could become a big star. Already, he shone on the field. But the pressure was on to keep playing well, and to make a successful baseball career.

José Reyes forces Barry Bonds out on second base during a game against the San Francisco Giants.

More Seasons with the Mets

Reyes was just getting started with the Mets. They seemed like a good team for him, too. With the Mets, his playing kept getting better.

The next year, 2007, was just as good as the year before. Again, no other player in the National League stole more bases that year. Reyes led the National League in stolen bases for three years in a row.

In December 2007, Reyes fans were happy to hear that he'd be on the cover of a video game. Reyes would be on the cover for *Major League Baseball 2K8* in 2008. Not many baseball players get to be on the cover of a game! He was chosen out of all the players in baseball.

There were more milestones in the years ahead. In September 2008, Reyes broke the Mets' record for stolen bases. Reyes had stolen more bases than any

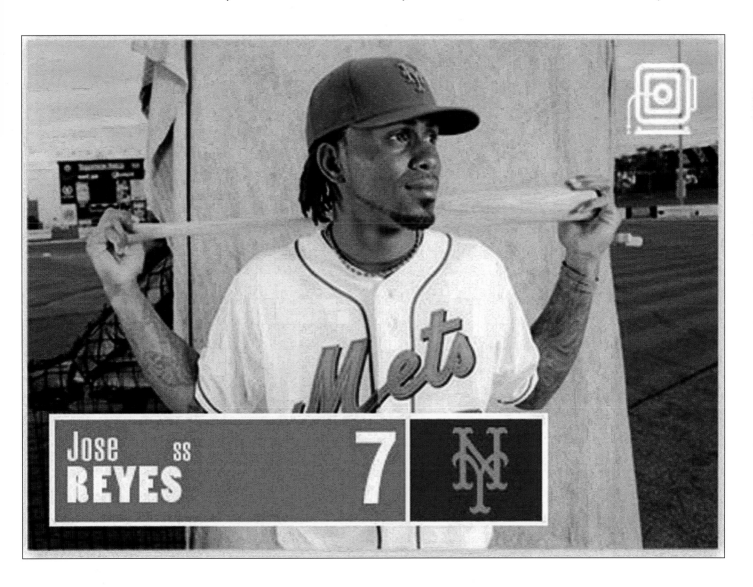

Reyes has had several injuries.

other Mets player in history. Stealing bases wasn't the only thing he was doing well, though. Pretty much everything he did, he did well.

A Hard Year

Since his start in professional baseball, Reyes had been on fire. Finally, in 2009, he hit a snag. In May, Reyes hurt his leg. No player wants to get a serious injury. Even if you're at the top of your game, an injury can bring you down. You can't use your talents, and you can't maintain the level of playing you're at because you can't practice. That's exactly what happened to Reyes.

At first, Reyes couldn't play at all. He worked hard to get better. He thought he might be ready to play in June. But then he hurt his leg again. Doctors checked Reyes' leg and found that he now had two different injuries. Then, he got hurt again while working out in August. Reyes didn't get to play much at all in 2009 because of his injuries.

After a very hard year in 2009, Reyes was ready to get back to baseball in 2010. His leg had healed, and he was eager to start playing again. But all that didn't matter at first. Before the season started, doctors found that Reyes was sick. They said he couldn't play. Reyes missed the start of the 2010 regular season.

When he finally got started, though, Reyes played well. His playing went right back to where it had been before he was injured. He hadn't let his time off get in his way.

Reyes was again chosen to be part of the All-Star Game in 2010. But sadly, Reyes couldn't play in the game. He got hurt again just before the All-Star game. Reyes went to the game with his family, instead, to watch.

These last couple of years had been tough for Reyes. He knew he could be a great baseball player, if he could only get healthy again. Luckily, he would have his chance again.

Chapter 5

JOSÉ REYES TODAY

In 2011, Reyes had another big year. The season was the last of his contract with the Mets. Fans wondered whether 2011 would be Reyes' last year in New York. Maybe he'd stay on the team longer, they thought. Even though many people talked about him in 2011 (and not always good things), Reyes didn't let that keep him from having a great season.

Another Successful Year

Reyes was chosen to be in the All-Star Game again in 2011. But he hurt his leg and wasn't able to play. Reyes didn't let his injury stop him from playing well for the rest of the season though.

One of his accomplishments that season was his high batting average. At .337, no other player in the National League had a higher batting average. Reyes was the National League Batting Champion of the 2011 season. Reyes's average was not just the best in the National League. His .337 batting average was the best of any year he'd had in Major League Baseball.

After the season was over, Reyes' contract with the Mets ended. He was a free agent. In December, he told his fans he'd be moving from New York. He wanted a change, and he wanted to get to the World Series.

Like a lot of Dominican baseball players, Reyes helps kids back home.

Reyes announced that he was moving to the Miami Marlins. He signed a six-year contract with the team. The team agreed to pay him $105 million over six seasons.

Reyes was leaving the team that had brought him into baseball. He'd only ever played with the Mets in the Majors. But it was time for Reyes to move on. He was excited about playing for the Marlins.

"It's a perfect situation in Miami," he told reporters. "We have the talent, a new stadium, and the city of Miami." Reyes was also wearing the new Marlins uniform for 2012. Miami fans were excited to see Reyes join the Marlins.

What's Next?

Baseball isn't the only thing that matters to Reyes. His family is very important to him. Reyes lives with his wife Katherine. The couple has three daughters. "There is nothing better than being a father," Reyes has said.

Reyes also remembers his roots. He remembers what he learned from his parents and stays close with them today. Remembering how much they gave him when he was young, Reyes gave his parents a house. But it wasn't just any house. He drove them out to a multi-million dollar Long Island house. Then he announced that they were home. His parents were stunned!

Reyes is also close to his home country. He's played for the Dominican Republic in the World Baseball Classic twice. Reyes may be a big star, but he hasn't forgotten where he came from.

Reyes also loves music. He's recorded some reggaeton songs. He's even got his own record company that sells his music. Reyes calls his company El7. Reyes loves baseball, but he also likes to make music on the side.

In 2011, he was featured in a hip-hop song called "No Hay Amigo." The song is about Reyes' childhood and the struggles he faced moving out of poverty and becoming a baseball player. He said, "I believe that everything I went through since [I was] a kid up until where I am at now, you understand that all the effort you put forward is all worth it when you're a kid, work hard every day without caring what other people say."

And if he doesn't have enough to do between baseball, his family, and music, Reyes also does charity work. For example, he renovated his hometown baseball field where he played when he was young. To do it, he started a chapter of Reviving Baseball in Inner cities (RBI), an MLB program that helps kids who otherwise couldn't play baseball.

2011 was Reyes' last year with the Mets.

José gives his dreads to charity.

RBI Program

The MLB is committed to charity work. It has lots of programs that give back, including the Reviving Baseball in Inner cities (RBI) program. RBI was started in 1989. Today, local programs are found in 200 cities. It helps 200,000 people every year. RBI does a lot. It renovates fields and ballparks. It has set up leagues for kids of all ages, to give them a chance to play on a real baseball or softball team. It also gives out scholarships for teens who finish high school and want to go on to college. There is even an RBI World Series.

Right before Reyes started playing with the Marlins, he also cut off all his hair for charity. He had always been known for his long dreadlocks, but the Marlins don't allow their players to have long hair. Instead of complaining, Reyes cut them off. Then he auctioned them off on eBay and gave the money to the Make-a-Wish Foundation, which makes lives better for kids with long-term illnesses.

Reyes may have done amazing things in baseball, but he still has goals to reach. Reyes hasn't won a World Series, for example. He's never even gotten to play in a World Series game! Reyes still has home runs to hit and bases to steal. He still has games to win and runs to score.

No matter what happens next for José Reyes, one thing is for sure. He'll work as hard as he can to be the best player he can be.

Find Out More

Online

Baseball Almanac
www.baseball-almanac.com

History of Baseball
www.19cbaseball.com

Baseball Hall of Fame
baseballhall.org

Major League Baseball
www.mlb.com

Baseball Reference
www.baseball-reference.com

Science of Baseball
www.exploratorium.edu/baseball

Dominican Baseball
mlb.mlb.com/mlb/features/dr/
index.jsp

In Books

Augustin, Bryan. *The Dominican Republic From A to Z.* New York: Scholastic, 2005.

Jacobs, Greg. *The Everything Kids' Baseball Book.* Avon, Mass.: F+W Media, 2012.

Kurlansky, Mark. *The Eastern Stars: How Baseball Changed the Dominican Town of San Pedro de Macorís.* New York: Riverhead Books, 2010.

Glossary

All-Star Game: The game played in July between the best players from each of the two leagues within the MLB.

batting average: A statistic that measures how good a batter is, which is calculated by dividing the number of hits a player gets by how many times he is at bat.

contract: A written promise between a player and the team. It tells how much he will be paid for how long.

culture: The way of life of a group of people, which includes things like values and beliefs, language, food, and art.

division: A group of teams that plays one another to compete for the championship; in the MLB, divisions are based on geographic regions.

free agent: A player who does not currently have a contract with any team.

Major League Baseball (MLB): The highest level of professional baseball in the United States and Canada.

minor leagues: The level of professional baseball right below the Major Leagues.

professional: The level of baseball in which players get paid.

scouts: People who find the best young baseball players to sign to teams.

sign: To agree to a contract between a baseball player and a team.

World Series: The final championship game in the MLB.

Index